Soul Masala

Poems Stirred, Not Shaken

R. K. Revelli

/ BookLeaf
Publishing

India | USA | UK

Made with ❤ on the BookLeaf Publishing Platform
www.bookleafpub.in
www.bookleafpub.com

Dedication

To my parents,

Mr. Ramaiah Revelli (Retired Principal, and Renowned Telugu Poet) recipient of the "*Sukavi Bhushana*" Lifetime Achievement Award, The award states that he is the jewel among the best poets in Telugu language.
and **Mrs. Tara Revelli**, who, with endless patience and enduring love, raised five wonderfully different characters under one roof,

You both wove the very first—and finest—spices into my soul.
Your love has been my comfort, your laughter my music, and your quiet strength my foundation.
Thank you for believing in my dreams—no matter how wild, funny, or poetic they seemed.
May every word in this book carry forward the warmth, wisdom, and vibrant spirit you instilled in me.

With all my love.

Preface

"Soul Masala" was born from small, everyday sparks: an overheard joke in a crowded lane, the wisdom in my father's one-liners, and my mother's advice—peppered with warmth, frustration, and, sometimes, a little masala of her own.

It finds flavor in my wife **Mrs. Padmaja**'s culinary expertise, whose hands create magic in our kitchen and whose recipes inspire both comfort and adventure. And it is brightened by my daughter **Ms. Keerthana**'s fearless kitchen experiments, where each new twist or surprise brings laughter and invention to our family table.

I wrote these poems for those facing storms and long roads, for those whose dreams sometimes feel like an inside joke, and for anyone who's ever danced in the kitchen with hope and a little madness.

This book is both a celebration and a rescue mission—an invitation to laugh at ourselves, to cherish humble beginnings, and to remember that there's flavor in every struggle. From Indian gullies to world stages, may these poems stir up courage, spice up slumps, and add a dash of delight to your day—without ever shaking your faith in brighter tomorrows.

Acknowledgements

With a grateful heart, I wish to thank:

My parents: Your boundless love and endless stories are the secret ingredients in every line I write.

My family and friends: Thank you for embracing my sudden fits of rhyme, late-night laughter, and masala-laden experiments—some delightful, some, let's admit, better left unserved!

My teachers and mentors: You taught me that words can heal wounds, humor can build bridges, and poetry, in its most honest form, can truly transform destinies.

Dear reader: Your openness to taste something bold, spicy, and a little unconventional gives me the courage to keep stirring joy, wisdom, and mischief into every verse. If you stumble upon a misstep, a spice too strong, or a line that missed its measure, I ask for your understanding and welcome your gentle corrections—they are recipes for making the next book even better.

To everyone who generously offered a poem, a smile, or a story along the way—thank you for seasoning my soul. Your suggestions, like the best recipes, are always cherished.

Best regards,
R.K.Revelli / rk.revelli@gmail.com

1. Breaking Dawn with Ginger Tea

Sun peeks bright, the world feels free,
Steam lifts hope in ginger tea.
Old fears fade with morning's plea,
Dreams swirl warm, just let them be.
Bitterness gone, possibility,
Laughter rising quietly.
Sip each breath, taste victory,
Eyes awake to what might be.
Kids run wild, birds agree,
Spice of life brewed easily.
Tired hearts find jubilee,
A brand new start is the key.
Worries hushed—so sip with me,
Begin again with ginger tea.

2. Spice Up Your Struggles

Troubles come, they always see,
Test your grin and guarantee.
Add some spice and let it be,
Mix the mess with energy.
Laugh it out, the recipe,
Wonder grows from misery.
Tears will salt your memory,
Rise again, unexpectedly.
Grit and punch bring harmony,
Patience slow as bamboo tree.
Every try sows legacy,
Savor now, set struggle free.
Every fall's a jubilee—
Spice your step, walk regally.

3. Laughing in the Monsoon Lane

Raindrops tap the windowpane,
Skipping puddles, joy again.
Boots that leap, forget the pain,
Trouble swirls then circles drain.
Giggles bubble, no refrain,
Umbrellas spin their own refrain.
Storms invite a fun campaign,
Friends all soaked, but none complain.
Every drop, a sweet champagne,
Memories wash, bold and plain.
Tales arise like sugarcane,
Smiles shine bright despite the rain.
Sorrow swept down every lane—
We laugh through life's monsoon rain.

4. The Chilli in My Courage

Tickle heat where doubts remain,
Chilli burns but breaks the chain.
Boldness blooms with pinch of pain,
Fire inside I can't restrain.
Fears dissolve in spicy vein,
Strength grows fierce with no disdain.
Sweat and grit in my campaign,
Courage dances, never tame.
Hurdles leap, I stake my claim,
Victory's sauce, never plain.
Failures spice the whole domain,
Growth and hope from what I gain.
Every scar's a red-hot stain—
I shine with chilli in my vein.

5. Turbulent Tuesdays and Turmeric Tips

Tuesday twirls, a hectic lane,
Deadlines dash but dreams remain.
Golden root to calm my brain,
Turmeric tea for peace I gain.
Chaos melts like summer rain,
Gentle sips, the worry's slain.
Yellow warmth through every vein,
Eases aches and soothes the strain.
Routines bright, never mundane,
Small advice in wisdom's chain.
Find the good, let stress be vain,
In every mug, comfort reign.
Little rituals entertain—
I rise with turmeric's refrain.

6. Salted Wounds, Sweet Recoveries

Tears that sting like ocean spray,
Salt the wounds that won't decay.
Pain runs deep but fades away,
Time heals what we cannot say.
Scars become our resume,
Stories told in yesterday.
Sweet recovery finds its way,
Through the hurt we thought would stay.
Hope returns like break of day,
Wounds transform to wisdom's ray.
What once broke now leads the way,
Stronger souls from yesterday.
Every fall becomes our bay—
Salt to sweet, our healing way.

7. Pepper for Your Purpose

Dreams need spice to come alive,
Pepper kicks to help them thrive.
Purpose burns when you arrive,
Goals ignite, your soul will drive.
Bland ambitions barely survive,
Add some heat, watch hope derive.
Passion's flame will help you strive,
Keep your vision sharp and jive.
Sneeze away what holds you back,
Fire fuels what others lack.
Purpose seasoned stays on track,
Bold moves keep you in the pack.
Pepper dreams with fearless zest—
Spicy goals will pass every test.

8. Masala Memories from the Corner Store

Dusty shelves and faded signs,
Uncle's smile in checkout lines.
Cardamom pods in neat designs,
Childhood joy in simple finds.
Every spice jar story tells,
Of mama's cooking, festival bells.
Corner store where memory dwells,
Sweet and salty, hopes and spells.
Turmeric stains on little hands,
Building dreams with rubber bands.
Simple moments, life's best plans,
Growing up where friendship stands.
Corner store, my heart's retreat—
Masala memories, bitter-sweet.

9. Dancing with Doubt and Cardamom

Doubt creeps in like morning mist,
Cardamom pods in my fist.
Sweet and bitter coexist,
Faith and fear cannot resist.
Dance with worry, take a turn,
Let the spices help you learn.
Confidence will slowly burn,
Trust in self, let courage churn.
Green pods crack, release their song,
Doubt was weak, but you are strong.
Dance with fear, it won't last long,
Find your rhythm, right your wrong.
Cardamom whispers, "You belong"—
Dance with doubt, but dance along.

10. Sambar for the Soul

Warm and rich, the comfort flows,
Like a hug when sorrow grows.
Tamarind tang that soothes and glows,
Simple love that always shows.
Lentils soft like mother's care,
Vegetables beyond compare.
Comfort found in what we share,
Soul food floating in the air.
Every spoonful tells a tale,
Of love that will never fail.
Home-cooked warmth when spirits pale,
Sambar comfort without fail.
Soul needs feeding, heart needs whole—
Sambar love for every soul.

11. Jugaad: The Art of Indian Ingenuity

Fix it up with what you've got,
Make it work, give all you've got.
Broken things need not be bought,
Creativity can't be taught.
Wire and tape, a clever mind,
Solutions that others cannot find.
Jugaad magic, one of a kind,
Leave perfection far behind.
Make do, make new, make it last,
Innovation unsurpassed.
Present born from creative past,
Ingenuity holds us fast.
Indian spirit, smart and free—
Jugaad is our legacy.

12. Curry Leaves in the Wind

Fragrant whispers on the breeze,
Curry leaves dance with such ease.
Memories float through the trees,
Childhood comfort that won't cease.
Green and fresh, they tell their story,
Of simple joys and homemade glory.
Flavors wrapped in allegory,
Each leaf holds our territory.
Wind carries what we hold dear,
Scents that bring our loved ones near.
Past and present crystal clear,
In every leaf, a happy tear.
Let the wind carry your dreams—
Like curry leaves in golden streams.

13. Who Stirred My Dreams?

Someone mixed my hopes around,
Dreams now floating, newly found.
What was lost has been unbound,
Clarity in every sound.
Who stirred magic in my cup?
Woke my spirit, stirred me up?
Changed my luck from down to up,
Filled my empty, broken cup.
Maybe life's the gentle hand,
Stirring dreams I hadn't planned.
Future bright, I take my stand,
Dreams now stirred across the land.
Grateful for the mystery—
Who stirred dreams inside of me?

14. The Rasam of Resilience

Sour days need pepper's bite,
Rasam soothes and makes things right.
Tangy broth, a healing sight,
Warms the soul from dark to light.
Tamarind teaches how to bend,
Not to break but to transcend.
Sour moments have their end,
Resilience, our truest friend.
Every storm will pass away,
Like the clouds on a rainy day.
Strength returns in every way,
Rasam wisdom here to stay.
Sip resilience, taste the gold—
Let your spirit be consoled.

15. Never a Dull Dal

Yellow comfort, simple fare,
Humble lentils beyond compare.
Life's like dal, we always care,
Basic goodness everywhere.
Some days thick, some days thin,
Consistency from deep within.
Dal reminds us where we've been,
Simple joys where life begins.
Never boring, always true,
Comfort comes in golden hue.
Basic things will see you through,
Simple pleasures, fresh and new.
In the ordinary, magic lies—
Never dull beneath the skies.

16. Paneer on the Move

Soft and firm, adaptable,
Paneer's spirit, capable.
Every dish, it's suitable,
Life lessons, quite notable.
Blend with others, keep your core,
Flexibility opens every door.
Change your shape but nothing more,
Stay yourself through every war.
Paneer wisdom, fresh and white,
Adapt to darkness, shine in light.
Keep your essence burning bright,
Move with grace, stand up and fight.
Be like paneer, strong yet mild—
Adaptable, yet unreciled.

17. Samosa Lessons: Wrapped and Ready

Crispy outside, warm within,
Samosa teaches where to begin.
Protect your heart, but let love in,
Golden layers, thick and thin.
Life's ingredients, mixed with care,
Folded tight with love to share.
Corners sharp but always fair,
Ready for what life might dare.
Hot oil tested, courage tried,
Golden brown with humble pride.
Crispy shell, soft heart inside,
Ready for whatever ride.
Wrapped and ready, stand your ground—
Best lessons in triangles found.

18. Hope Served Hot

Steam rises with the morning sun,
Hope served hot for everyone.
Yesterday's worries, now undone,
A brand new day has just begun.
Warmth spreads through the coldest heart,
Hope gives every soul fresh start.
Never let your dreams depart,
Hope's the most essential art.
Served fresh daily, never stale,
Hope will help you tell your tale.
When your strength begins to fail,
Hope served hot will never pale.
Order up and take your share—
Hope served hot is everywhere.

19. Pickles of Perseverance

Sour times need extra time,
Like pickles aging, slow sublime.
Patience mixed with salty rhyme,
Preserved through every uphill climb.
Oil of effort, spices bold,
Stories that will never get old.
Tangy trials make us bold,
Worth much more than liquid gold.
Every jar holds memories,
Of struggles faced and victories.
Pickled pain and victories,
Time transforms our histories.
Preserved through seasons, sweet and sour—
Perseverance is our power.

20. Moonlit Madness and Mango Magic

Moonbeams dance on mango trees,
Night whispers carried on the breeze.
Madness mixed with memories,
Sweet magic that will never cease.
Yellow dreams and silver light,
Stars that make the darkness bright.
Mango sweetness through the night,
Everything will be alright.
Crazy moments under stars,
Healing all our hidden scars.
Moon and mango, near and far,
Magic's always where you are.
Let the moonlight make you free—
Mango magic, wild and free.

21. The Final Recipe: Finding Your Flavor

Every spice has found its place,
Every story shows your grace.
Final recipe, embrace,
Your own unique and special taste.
Mix the lessons, stir them well,
Stories only you can tell.
In your flavor, you excel,
Ring your own success bell.
You're the chef, you hold the spoon,
Life's your kitchen, find your tune.
Morning, evening, night and noon,
Your flavor's perfectly in tune.
Cook with love, season with dreams—
Your recipe's better than it seems.